THE NEGRO PROTEST

THE NEGRO PROTEST

James Baldwin

Malcolm X

Martin Luther King

talk with
Kenneth B. Clark

BEACON PRESS   BOSTON

*The interviews in this book were produced for
National Educational Television by WGBH-TV, Boston:
Henry Morgenthau III, Producer; Mary Rose Maybank,
Co-Producer; Fred Barzyk, Director.*

CONTENTS

James Baldwin

talks with

Kenneth B. Clark

The following interview with James Baldwin occurred under extraordinary circumstances. We were scheduled to be at the television studio at 5:00 P.M. on Friday, May 24, 1963, the day of the well-publicized meeting between Attorney General Robert Kennedy and James Baldwin and some of his friends. The meeting had aroused in all of us an intense level of emotions. The seeming inability to communicate the passionate insistence of Mr. Baldwin that the Attorney General *had* to understand the sense of urgency of the Negro people, and the need of the Attorney General to protect the image of liberal concern within the context of political realism had contributed to an excruciating sense of impasse. The meeting continued for nearly three hours, and resulted in Mr. Baldwin's and my being an hour and a half late for the taping of the interview. On the way to the studio, it was clear that the emotionality and general sense of frustration resulting from the meeting with the Attorney General would be carried over into the interview. Indeed, many times in the taxicab, Baldwin said that he was not sure that he would be able to go through with the interview. He stated repeatedly, "Kenneth, all I need is a drink. Can't we stop at the nearest bar? I must decompress."

Literally, there was no time either to prepare questions or to discuss generally what course the interview would take. When we reached the studio the cameraman and technicians were understandably impatient. We were placed immediately in our chairs while they set up the cameras for proper angles, lighting, and determined the voice levels. During this brief interval, Baldwin and I merely had time to reassure each other that we did not know exactly what we were going to talk about. The interview which follows is purely spontaneous, and in the

trite words of television, "completely (but completely) unre-
hearsed." In fact, neither Baldwin nor I was quite sure of what
we had actually said during the interview immediately after-
ward or in the following weeks. We were unable to recall either
specific questions and answers, or general trends. We were
sure only of the mood and the fact that the interview was in
someway dominated by our earlier experience with the Attorney General. We thought that we had probably devoted the
entire interview to a rehashing of that meeting.

James Baldwin is a little man, physically, with tremendous
emotional and intellectual power. He radiates a nervous, sensitive involvement with all aspects of his environment. One has the
impression that he speaks with his entire body. His ideas, his
feelings, and his words appear to form a complete unity. In his
conversations he is the essence of spontaneity and one has the
impression that he is incapable of communicating anything
other than the total truth which he feels and thinks at that
particular time. I began our interview by asking Baldwin about
his childhood, and given the circumstances it is not surprising
that he replied:

What a funny question! My mind is some
place else, really; but to think back on it—I was born in
Harlem, Harlem Hospital, and we grew up—the first house
I remember was on Park Avenue, which is not the American
Park Avenue, or maybe it *is* the American Park Avenue.

CLARK: Uptown Park Avenue.

BALDWIN: Uptown Park Avenue, where the railroad
tracks are. We used to play on the roof and in the—I can't
call it an alley—but near the river—it was a kind of dump,
a garbage dump. That was the first—those were the first
scenes I remember. I remember my father had trouble keep-
ing us alive; there were nine of us. And I was the oldest so
I took care of the kids and dealt with Daddy. I understand

him much better now. Part of his problem was he couldn't feed his kids, but I was a kid and I didn't know that. And he was very religious and very rigid. He kept us together, I must say. And when I look back on it—after all it was nearly forty years ago that I was born—when I think back on my growing up and walk that same block today, because it's still there, and think of the kids on that block now, I'm aware that something terrible has happened which is very hard to describe. I am, in all but in technical legal fact, a Southerner. My father was born in the South—no, my mother was born in the South, and if they had waited two more seconds I might have been born in the South. But that means I was raised by families whose roots were essentially rural——

CLARK: Southern rural.

BALDWIN: Southern rural and whose relationship to the church was very direct because it was the only means they had of expressing their pain and their despair. But twenty years later the moral authority which was present in the Negro Northern community when I was growing up has vanished. And people talk about progress, and I look at Harlem which I really know—I know it like I know my hand—and it is much worse there today than it was when I was growing up.

CLARK: Would you say this is true of the schools too?

BALDWIN: It is much worse in the schools.

CLARK: What school did you go to?

BALDWIN: I went to P.S. 24 and I went to P.S. 139.

CLARK: We are fellow alumni. I went to 139.

BALDWIN: I didn't like a lot of my teachers, but I had a couple of teachers who were very nice to me; one was a Negro teacher. And I remember—you ask me these questions and I'm trying to answer you—I remember coming home from school, you can guess how young I must have been, and my mother asked me if my teacher was colored or white, and I said she was a little bit colored and a little bit white, but she was about your color. And as a matter of fact I was right. That's part of the dilemma of being an American Negro; that one is a little bit colored and a little bit white, and not only in physical terms but in the head and in the heart, and there are days—this is one of them—when you wonder what your role is in this country and what your future is in it; how precisely you are going to reconcile it to your situation here and how you are going to communicate to the vast heedless, unthinking, cruel white majority, that you are here. And to be here means that you can't be anywhere else. I could, my own person, leave this country and go to Africa, I could go to China, I could go to Russia, I could go to Cuba, but I'm an American and that is a *fact.*

CLARK: Yes. Jim——

BALDWIN: Am I going ahead?

CLARK: No, these are certainly some of the things that we are after, but as I read your writings and know that you came out of P.S. 24 and my alma mater, Junior High School 139, I see that no one could write with the feeling and with the skill with which you write if you did not get, in P.S. 24 and 139, a certain type of education. Now I'd like to go back to the point that you made that the Harlem that you knew when you were growing up is not the Harlem now and see if we can relate this also even to the school.

BALDWIN: Let's see. Let's see if we can. It was probably very important for me—I haven't thought of this for a long time—it was important at the point I was going to P.S. 24—the only Negro school principal as far as I know in the entire history of New York was the principal—a woman named Mrs. Ayer, and she liked me. And in a way I guess she proved to me that I didn't have to be entirely defined by my circumstances, because you know that every Negro child knows what his circumstances are though he can't articulate them, because he is born into a republic which assures him in as many ways as it knows how, and has got great force, that he has a certain place and he can never rise above it. And what has happened in Harlem since is that that generation has passed away.

CLARK: Mrs. Ayer was a sort of a model in a sense.

BALDWIN: She was a proof. She was a living proof that I was not necessarily what the country said I was.

CLARK: Then it is significant, Jim, that we do not have a single Negro principal in the New York public school system today.

BALDWIN: And it is *not* because "there ain't nobody around who can do it," you know. One's involved in a very curious and a very serious battle concerning which I think the time has come to be as explicit as one can possibly be. The great victims in this country of an institution called segregation (it is not a southern custom but has been for a hundred years a national way of life) the great victims are white people, the white man's children. Lorraine Hansberry said this afternoon—we were talking about the problem of being a Negro male in this society—Lorraine said she wasn't too concerned really about Negro manhood since they had managed to endure and to even transcend some fantastic things, but she was very worried about a civilization which could produce those five policemen standing on the Negro woman's neck in Birmingham or wherever it was, and I am too. I'm terrified at the moral apathy, the death of the heart, which is happening in my country. These people have deluded themselves for so long that they really don't think I'm human. I base this on their conduct, not on what they say, and this means that they have become in themselves moral monsters. It's a terrible indictment. I mean every word I say.

CLARK: Well, we are confronted with the racial confrontation in America today. I think the pictures of dogs in the hands of human beings attacking other human beings——

BALDWIN: In a free country—in the middle of the twentieth century.

CLARK: This Birmingham is clearly not restricted to Birmingham as you so eloquently pointed out. What do you think can be done to change, to use your term, the moral fiber of America?

BALDWIN: I think that one has got to find some way of putting the present administration of this country on the spot. One has got to force, somehow, from Washington, a moral commitment, not to the Negro people, but to the life of this country. It doesn't matter any longer—and I'm speaking for myself, Jimmy Baldwin, and I think I'm speaking for a great many other Negroes too—it doesn't matter any longer what you do to me; you can put me in jail, you can kill me. By the time I was seventeen, you'd done everything that you could do to me. The problem now is how are you going to save yourselves? It was a great shock to me—I want to say this on the air—the Attorney General did not know——

CLARK: You mean the Attorney General of the United States?

BALDWIN: Mister Robert Kennedy—didn't know that I would have trouble convincing my nephew to go to Cuba, for example, to liberate the Cubans in defense of a government which now says it is doing everything it can do, which cannot liberate me. Now, there are twenty million Negroes in this country, and you can't put them all in jail. I know how my nephew feels, I know how I feel, I know how the cats in the barbershop feel. A boy last week, he was sixteen, in San Francisco told me on television—thank God, we got him to talk, maybe somebody else ought to listen—he said, "I got no country. I got no flag." Now, he's only sixteen years old, and I couldn't say, "You do." I don't have any evidence to prove that he does. They were tearing down his house, because San Francisco is engaging, as most Northern cities now are engaged, in something called urban renewal, which means moving Negroes out; it means Negro removal, that is what it means. And the federal government is an accomplice to this fact. Now, we are talking about human beings; there's not such a thing as a monolithic wall or some abstraction called the Negro problem; these are Negro boys and girls, who at sixteen and seventeen don't believe the country means anything that it says and don't feel they have any place here on the basis of the performance of the entire country.

CLARK: But now, Jim——

BALDWIN: Am I exaggerating?

CLARK: No, I certainly could not say that you are exaggerating, but there is this picture of a group of young Negro college students in the South coming from colleges where the whole system seems to conspire to keep them from having courage, integrity, clarity and the willingness to take the risks which they have been taking for these last three or four years. Could you react to the student non-violent movement which has made such an impact on America, which has affected both Negroes and whites and seems to have jolted them out of the lethargy of tokenism and moderation? How do you account for this, Jim?

BALDWIN: Well, of course, one of the things I think that happened, Ken, really, is that in the first place, the Negro has never been as docile as white Americans wanted to believe. That was a myth. We were not singing and dancing down on the levee. We were trying to keep alive; we were trying to survive a very brutal system. The Negro has never been happy in "his" place. What those kids first of all proved —first of all they proved *that*. They come from a long line of fighters. And what they also prove—I want to get to your point, really—what they also prove is not that the Negro has changed, but that the country has arrived at a place where he can no longer contain the revolt. He can no longer, as he could do once—let's say I was a Negro college president, and I needed a new chemistry lab., so I was a Negro leader. I was a Negro leader because the white man said I was, and I came to get a new chemistry lab., "Please, suh," and the tacit price I paid for the chemistry lab. was controlled by the people I represented. And now I can't do that. When the boy said this afternoon—we were talking to a Negro student this afternoon who had been through it all, who's half dead and only about twenty-five. Jerome Smith. That's an awful lot to ask a person to bear. The country has sat back in admiration of all those kids for three or four or five years and has not lifted a finger to help them. Now, we all knew. I know you knew and I knew, too, that a moment was coming when we couldn't guarantee, that no one can guarantee, that he won't reach the breaking point. You can only survive so many beatings, so much humiliation, so much despair, so many broken promises, before something gives. Human beings are not by nature non-violent. Those children had to pay a terrible price in discipline, moral discipline, an interior effort of courage which the country cannot imagine, because it still thinks Gary Cooper, for example, was a man. I mean his image—I have nothing against him, you know, *him*.

CLARK: You said something, that you cannot expect them to remain constantly non-violent.

BALDWIN: No, you can't! You can't! And, furthermore, they were always, these students that we are talking about, a minority—the students we are talking about, not in Tal-lahassee. There were some students protesting, but there were many, many, many, many more students who had given up, who were desperate and whom Malcolm X can reach, for example, much more easily than I can.

CLARK: What do you mean?

BALDWIN: Well, Malcolm tells them—what Malcolm tells them, in effect, is that they should be proud of being black, and God knows that they should be. That is a very impor-tant thing to hear in a country which assures you that you should be ashamed of it. Of course, in order to do this, what he does is destroy a truth and invent a history. What he does is say, "You're better *because* you're black." Well, of course that isn't true. That's the trouble.

CLARK: Do you think this is an appealing approach and that the Black Muslims in preaching black supremacy seek to exploit the frustration of the Negro?

BALDWIN: I don't think, to put it as simply as I can, and without trying now to investigate whatever the motives of any given Muslim leader may be. It is the only movement in the country that you can call grass roots. I hate to say that, but it's true. Because it is the only—when Malcolm talks or the Muslim ministers talk, they articulate for all the Negro people who hear them, who listen to them. They articulate their suffering, the suffering which has been in this country so long denied. That's Malcolm's great authority over any of his audiences. He corroborates their reality; he tells them that they really exist.

CLARK: Jim, do you think that this is a more effective ap-peal than the appeal of Martin Luther King?

BALDWIN: It is much more sinister because it is much more effective. It is much more effective, because it is, after all, comparatively easy to invest a population with false morale by giving them a false sense of superiority, and it will always break down in a crisis. That's the history of Europe simply; it's one of the reasons that we are in this terrible place. It is one of the reasons that we have five cops standing on the black woman's neck in Birmingham, because at some point they believed, they were taught and they *believed* that they were better than other people because they were white. It leads to moral bankruptcy. It is inevitable, it cannot but lead there. But my point here is that the country is for the first time worried about the Muslim movement. It shouldn't be worried about the Muslim movement, that's not the problem. The problem is to eliminate the conditions which breed the Muslim movement.

CLARK: I'd like to come back to get some of your thoughts about the relationship between Martin Luther King's appeal, that is, effectively, non-violence and his philosophy of disciplined love for the oppressor. What is the relationship between this and the reality of the Negro masses?

BALDWIN: Well, to leave Martin out of it for a moment. Martin's a very rare, a very great man. Martin's rare for two reasons: probably just because he *is;* and because he's a real Christian. He really believes in non-violence. He has arrived at something in himself which permits him—allows him to do it, and he still has great moral authority in the South. He has none whatever in the North. Poor Martin has gone through God knows what kind of hell to awaken the American conscience, but Martin has reached the end of his rope. There are some things Martin can't do; Martin's only one man. Martin can't solve the nations' central problem by himself. There are lots of people, lots of black people I mean, now, who "don't go to church no more" and don't listen to Martin, you know, and who anyway are themselves produced by a civilization which has always glorified violence unless the Negro has the gun so that Martin is undercut by the performance of the country. The country is only concerned about non-violence if it seems as if I'm going to get violent, because I worry about non-violence if it's some Alabama sheriff.

CLARK: Jim, what do you see deep in the recesses of your own mind as the future of our nation, and I ask that question in that way because I think that the future of the Negro and the future of the nation are linked.

BALDWIN: They're insoluble.

CLARK: Now, how—what do you see? Are you essentially optimistic or pessimistic? And I don't really want to put words in your mouth because what I really want to find out is what you really believe.

BALDWIN: I'm both glad and sorry you asked me that question, but I'll do my best to answer it. I can't be a pessimist because I'm alive. To be a pessimist means that you have agreed that human life is an academic matter, so I'm forced to be an optimist; I'm forced to believe that we can survive whatever we must survive. But the future of the Negro in this country is precisely as bright or as dark as the future of the country. It is entirely up to the American people and our representatives, it is entirely up to the American people whether or not they are going to face and deal with and embrace the stranger whom they maligned so long. What white people have to do is try to find out in their own hearts why it was necessary to have a nigger in the first place. Because I'm not a nigger, I am a man, but if you think I'm a nigger, it means you need it. The question you got to ask yourself—the white population has got to ask itself, North and South, because it's one country and for a Negro there's no difference between the North and South; there's just a difference in the way they castrate you, but the fact of the castration is the American fact. If I'm not the nigger here and if you invented him—you, the white people, invented him, then you've got to find out why. And the future of the country depends on that. Whether or not it's able to ask that question.

CLARK: As a Negro and an American, I can only hope that America has the strength——

BALDWIN: Moral strength.

CLARK: ——and the capacity to ask and answer that question——

BALDWIN: To *face* that question, to *face* that question!

CLARK: ——in an affirmative and constructive way.

Malcolm X

talks with

Kenneth B. Clark

Malcolm X is a punctual man. He arrived at the television studio, with two of his closest advisors, at the precise time of our appointment. He and his friends were immaculately dressed, with no outward sign of their belonging either to a separate sect or the ministry. Minister Malcolm X (and he insists upon being called "Minister Malcolm") is a tall, handsome man in his late thirties. He is clearly a dominant personality whose disciplined power seems all the more evident in contrast to the studied deference paid him by his associates. He is conscious of the impression of power which he seeks to convey, and one suspects that he does not permit himself to become too casual in his relations with others.

Although Minister Malcolm X seems proud of the fact that he did not go beyond the eighth grade, he speaks generally with the vocabulary and the tone of a college-educated person. Happy when this is pointed out to him, he explains that he has read extensively since joining the Black Muslim movement. His role as the chief spokesman for this movement in the New York-Washington region is, he insists, to raise the level of pride and accomplishment in his followers.

Malcolm X has been interviewed on radio, television, and by newspapermen probably more than any other Negro leader during the past two years. He shows the effects of these interminable interviews by a professional calm, and what appears to be an ability to turn on the proper amount of emotion, resentment, and indignation, as needed. One certainly does not get the impression of spontaneity. On the contrary, one has the feeling that Minister Malcolm has anticipated every question and is prepared with the appropriate answer, an answer which is consistent with the general position of the Black Muslim movement, as defined by the Honorable Elijah Muhammad.

We began the interview by talking about Malcom X's childhood:

I was born in Omaha, Nebraska, back in 1925, that period when the Ku Klux Klan was quite strong in that area at that time—and grew up in Michigan, partially. Went to school there.

CLARK: What part of Michigan?

MALCOLM X: Lansing. I went to school there—as far as the eighth grade. And left there and then grew up in Boston and in New York.

CLARK: Did you travel with your family from Omaha to Michigan to Boston?

MALCOLM X: Yes. When I was born—shortly after I was born—the Ku Klux Klan gave my father an ultimatum —or parents an ultimatum—about remaining there, so they left and went to——

CLARK: What was the basis of this ultimatum?

MALCOLM X: My father was a Garveyite, and in those days, you know, it wasn't the thing for a black man to be outspoken or to deviate from the accepted stereotype that was usually considered the right image for Negroes to fulfill or reflect.

CLARK: Of all the words that I have read about you, this is the first time that I've heard that your father was a Garveyite. And, in fact, he *was* an outspoken black nationalist in the nineteen-twenties?

MALCOLM X: He was both a Garveyite and a minister, a Baptist minister. In those days you know how it was and how it still is; it has only changed in the method, but the same things still exist: whenever a black man was outspoken, he was considered crazy or dangerous. And the police department and various branches of the law usually were interwoven with that Klan element, so the Klan had the backing of the police, and usually the police had the backing of the Klan, same as today.

CLARK: So in effect your father was required, or he was forced——

MALCOLM X: Yes, they burned the house that we lived in in Omaha, and I think this was in 1925, and we moved to Lansing, Michigan, and we ran into the same experience there. We lived in an integrated neighborhood, by the way, then. And it only proves that whites were as much against integration as they are now, only then they were more openly against it. And today they are shrewd in saying they are for it, but they still make it impossible for you to integrate. So we moved to Michigan and the same thing happened; they burned our home there. And he was—like I say—he was a clergyman, a Christian; and it was Christians who burned the home in both places—people who teach, you know, religious tolerance and brotherhood and all of them.

CLARK: Did you start school in Michigan?

MALCOLM X: Yes.

CLARK: How long did you stay in Michigan?

MALCOLM X: I think I completed the eighth grade while I was still in Michigan.

CLARK: And then where did you go?

MALCOLM X: To Boston.

CLARK: Did you go to high school in Boston?

MALCOLM X: No, I have never gone to high school.

CLARK: You've never gone to high school?

MALCOLM X: The eighth grade was as far as I went.

CLARK: That's phenomenal.

MALCOLM X: Everything I know above the eighth grade, I've learned from Mister Muhammad. He's been my teacher, and I think he's a better teacher than I would have had had I continued to go to the public schools.

CLARK: How did you meet Mister Muhammad?

MALCOLM X: I was—when I was in prison, in 1947, I first heard about his teaching; about his religious message. And at that time I was an atheist, myself. I had graduated from Christianity to agnosticism on into atheism.

CLARK: Were the early experiences in Nebraska and Michigan where, as you say, Christians burned the home of your father who was a Christian minister—were these experiences the determinants of your moving away from Christianity?

MALCOLM X: No, no, they weren't, because despite those experiences, I, as I said, lived a thoroughly integrated life. Despite all the experiences I had in coming up—and my father was killed by whites at a later date—I still thought that there were some good white people; at least the ones *I* was associating with, you know, were supposed to be different. There wasn't any experience, to my knowledge, that opened up my eyes, because right up until the time that I went to prison, I was still integrated into the white society and thought that there were some good ones.

CLARK: Was it an integrated prison?

MALCOLM X: It was an integrated prison at the prison level, but the administrators were all white. You usually find that in any situation that is supposed to be based on integration. At the low level they integrate, but at the administrative or executive level you find whites running it.

CLARK: How long did you stay in prison?

MALCOLM X: About seven years.

CLARK: And you were in prison in Boston. And this is where you got in touch with——

MALCOLM X: My family became Muslims; accepted the

religion of Islam, and one of them who had spent pretty much—had spent quite a bit of time with me on the streets of New York out here in Harlem had been exposed to the religion of Islam. He accepted it, and it made such a profound change in him. He wrote to me and was telling me about it. Well, I had completely eliminated Christianity. After getting into prison and having time to think, I could see the hypocrisy of Christianity. Even before I went to prison, I had already become an atheist and I could see the hypocrisy of Christianity. Most of my associates were white; they were either Jews or Christians, and I saw hypocrisy on both sides. None of them really practiced what they preached.

CLARK: Minister Malcolm——

MALCOLM X: Excuse me, but despite the fact that I had detected this, my own intellectual strength was so weak, or so lacking, till I was not in a position to really see or come to a conclusion concerning this hypocrisy until I had gotten to where I could think a little bit and had learned more about the religion of Islam. Then I could go back and remember all of these experiences and things that I had actually heard—discussions that I had participated in myself with whites. It had made everything that Mister Muhammad was saying add up.

CLARK: I see.

MALCOLM X: He was the one who drew the line and enabled me to add up everything and say that this is this, and I haven't met anyone since then who was capable of showing me an answer more strong or with more weight than the answer that the Honorable Elijah Muhammad has given.

CLARK: I'd like to go back just a little to your life in prison. What was the basis—how did you——

MALCOLM X: Crime. I wasn't framed. I went to prison

for what I did, and the reason that I don't have any hesitation or reluctance whatsoever to point out the fact that I went to prison: I firmly believe that it was the Christian society, as you call it, the Judaic-Christian society, that created all of the factors that send so many so-called Negroes to prison. And when these fellows go to prison there is nothing in the system designed to rehabilitate them. There's nothing in the system designed to reform them. All it does is—it's a breeding ground for more professional type of criminal, especially among Negroes. Since I saw, detected, the reluctance on the part of penologists, prison authorities, to reform men and even detected that—noticed that after a so-called Negro in prison trys to reform and become a better man, the prison authorities are more against *that* man than they were against him when he was completely criminally inclined, so this is again hypocrisy. Not only is the Christian society itself religious hypocrisy, but the court system is hypocrisy, the entire penal system is hypocrisy. Everything is hypocrisy. Mister Muhammad came along with his religious gospel and introduced the religion of Islam and showed the honesty of Islam, showed the justice in Islam, the freedom in Islam. Why naturally, just comparing the two, Christianity had already eliminated itself, so all I had to do was accept the religion of Islam. I know today what it has done for me as a person.

CLARK: I notice that the Black Muslim movement has put a great deal of time, effort and energy in seeking recruits within the prisons.

MALCOLM X: This is incorrect.

CLARK: It is incorrect?

MALCOLM X: It is *definitely* incorrect.

CLARK: Eric Lincoln's book——

MALCOLM X: Well, Lincoln is incorrect himself. Lincoln is just a Christian preacher from Atlanta, Georgia, who wanted to make some money, so he wrote a book and called it *The Black Muslims in America*. We're not even Black Muslims. We are black people in a sense that "black" is an adjective. We are black people who are Muslims because we have accepted the religion of Islam, but what Eric Lincoln shrewdly did was capitalize the letter "b," and made "black" an adjectival noun and then attached it to "Muslim," and now it is used by the press to make it appear that this is the name of an organization. It has no religious connotation or religious motivation or religious objectives.

CLARK: You do not have a systematic campaign for recruiting or rehabilitating?

MALCOLM X: No, no.

CLARK: What about rehabilitation?

MALCOLM X: The reason that the religion of Islam has spread so rapidly in prison is because the average so-called Negro in prison has had experiences enough to make him realize the hypocrisy of everything in this society, and he also has experienced the fact that the system itself is not designed to rehabilitate him or make him turn away from crime. Then when he hears the religious teaching of the Honorable Elijah Muhammad that restores to him his racial pride, his racial identity, and restores to him also the desire to be a man, to be a human being, he reforms himself. And this spreads so rapidly among the so-called Negroes in prison that, since the sociologist and the psychologists and the penologist and the criminologist have all realized their own inability to rehabilitate the criminal, when Mr. Muhammad comes along and starts rehabilitating the criminal with just the religious gospel, it's a miracle. They look upon it as a sociological phenomenon or psychological phenomena, and it gets great publicity.

CLARK: You do not, therefore, have to actively recruit.

MALCOLM X: The Honorable Elijah Muhammad has no

active effort to convert or recruit men in prison any more so than he does Negroes, period. I think that what you should realize, is that in America there are twenty million black people, all of whom are in prison. You don't have to go to Sing Sing to be in prison. If you're born in America with a black skin, you're born in prison, and the masses of black people in America today are beginning to regard our plight or predicament in this society as one of a prison inmate. And when they refer to the President, he's just another warden to whom they turn to open the cell door, but it's no different. It's the same thing, and just as the warden in the prison couldn't rehabilitate those men, the President in this country couldn't rehabilitate or change the thinking of the masses of black people. And as the Honorable Elijah Muhammad has been able to go behind the prison walls—the physical prison walls—and release those men from that which kept them criminals, he likewise on a mass scale throughout this country—he is able to send his religious message into the so-called Negro community and rehabilitate the thinking of our people and made them conquer the habits and the vices and the evils that have held us in the clutches of this white man's society.

CLARK: I think, Minister Malcolm, what you have just said brings me to trying to hear from you directly your ideas concerning the philosophy of the Black Muslim movement. Among the things that have been written about this movement, the things which stand out are the fact that this movement preaches hatred for whites; that it preaches black supremacy; that it, in fact, preaches, or if it does not directly preach, it accepts the inevitability of violence as a factor in the relationship between the races. Now——

MALCOLM X: That's a strange thing. You know, the Jews here in this city rioted last week against some Nazi, and I was listening to a program last night where the other Jew— where a Jewish commentator was congratulating what the

Jews did to this Nazi; complimenting them for it. Now no one mentioned violence in connection with what the Jews did against these Nazis. But these same Jews, who will condone violence on their part or hate someone whom they consider to be an enemy, will join Negro organizations and tell Negroes to be non-violent; that it is wrong or immoral, unethical, unintelligent for Negroes to reflect some kind of desire to defend themselves from the attacks of whites who are trying to brutalize us. The Muslims who follow the Honorable Elijah Muhammad don't advocate violence, but Mister Muhammad does teach us that any human being who is intelligent has the right to defend himself. You can't take a black man who is being bitten by dogs and accuse him of advocating violence because he trys to defend himself from bite of the dog. If you notice, the people who are sicking the dogs on the black people are never accused of violence; they are never accused of hate. Nothing like that is ever used in the context of a discussion when it's about them. It is only when the black man begins to explode and erupt after he has had too much that they say that the black man is violent, and as long as these whites are putting out a doctrine that paves the way to justify their mistreatment of blacks, this is never called hate. It is only when the black man himself begins to spell out the historic deeds of what whites have been doing to him in this country that the shrewd white man with his control over the news media and propaganda makes it appears that the black people today are advocating some kind of hate. Mr. Muhammad teaches us to love each other, and when I say love each other—love our own kind. This is all black people need to be taught in this country because the only ones whom we don't love are our own kind. Most of the Negroes you see running around here talking about "love everybody"—they don't have any love whatsoever for their own kind. When they say, "Love everybody," what they are doing is setting up a situation for

us to love white people. This is what their philosophy is. Or
when they say, "Suffer peacefully," they mean suffer peacefully at the hands of the white man, because the same non-
violent Negroes are the advocators of non-violence. If a
Negro attacks one of them, they'll fight that Negro all over
Harlem. It's only when the white man attacks them that they
believe in non-violence, all of them.

CLARK: Mister X, is this a criticism of the Reverend
Martin Luther King?

MALCOLM X: You don't have to criticize Reverend Martin
Luther King. His actions criticize him.

CLARK: What do you mean by this?

MALCOLM X: Any Negro who teaches other Negroes to
turn the other cheek is disarming that Negro. Any Negro
who teaches Negroes to turn the other cheek in the face of
attack is disarming that Negro of his God-given right, of his
moral right, of his natural right, of his intelligent right to
defend himself. Everything in nature can defend itself, and
is right in defending itself except the American Negro. And
men like King—their job is to go among Negroes and teach
Negroes "Don't fight back." He doesn't tell them, "Don't
fight each other." "Don't fight the white man" is what he's
saying in essence, because the followers of Martin Luther
King will cut each other from head to foot, but they will not
do anything to defend themselves against the attacks of the
white man. But King's philosophy falls upon the ears of
only a small minority. The majority or masses of black people in this country are more inclined in the direction of the
Honorable Elijah Muhammad than Martin Luther King.

CLARK: Is it not a fact though——

MALCOLM X: *White* people follow King. *White* people
pay King. *White* people subsidize King. *White* people support King. But the masses of black people don't support
Martin Luther King. King is the best weapon that the white

man, who wants to brutalize Negroes, has ever gotten in this country, because he is setting up a situation where, when the white man wants to attack Negroes, they can't defend themselves, because King has put this foolish philosophy out— you're not supposed to fight or you're not supposed to defend yourself.

CLARK: But Mister X, is it not a fact that Reverend King's movement was successful in Montgomery——

MALCOLM X: You can't tell me that you have had success —excuse me, sir.

CLARK: Was it not a success in Birmingham?

MALCOLM X: No, no. What kind of success did they get in Birmingham? A chance to sit at a lunch counter and drink some coffee with a cracker—that's success? A chance to— thousands of little children went to jail; they didn't get out, they were bonded out by King. They had to *pay* their way out of jail. That's not any kind of advancement or success.

CLARK: What *is* advancement from the point of view of the Muslims?

MALCOLM X: Any time dogs have bitten black women, bitten black children—when I say dogs, that is four-legged dogs and two-legged dogs have brutalized thousands of black people—and the one who advocates himself as their leader is satisfied in making a compromise or a deal with the same ones who did this to these people only if they will offer him a job, one job, downtown for one Negro or things of that sort, I don't see where there's any kind of success, sir; it's a sellout. Negroes in Birmingham are in worse condition now than they were then because the line is more tightly drawn. And to say that some moderate—to say that things are better now because a different man, a different white man, a different southern white man is in office now, who's supposed to be a moderate, is to tell me that you are better off dealing with a fox than you were when you were dealing with a wolf. The ones that they were dealing with previously were wolves, and they didn't hide the fact that they were wolves. The man that they got to deal with now is a fox, but he's no better than the wolf. Only he's better in his ability to lull the Negroes to sleep, and he'll do that as long as they listen to Doctor Martin Luther King.

CLARK: What would be the goals, or what are the goals of the Black Muslim movement? What would the Black Muslim movement insist upon in Birmingham, in Montgomery and in Jackson, Mississippi, et cetera?

MALCOLM X: Well, number one, the Honorable Elijah Muhammad teaches us that the solution will never be brought about by politicians, it will be brought about by God, and that the only way the black man in this country today can receive respect and recognition of other people is to stand on his own feet; get something for himself and do something for himself; and the solution that God has given the Honorable Elijah Muhammad is the same as the solution that God gave to Moses when the Hebrews in the Bible were in a predicament similar to the predicament of the so-called Negroes here in America today, which is nothing other than a modern house of bondage, or a modern Egypt, or a modern Babylon. And Moses' answer was to separate these slaves from their slave master and show the slaves how to go to a land of their own where they would serve a God of their own and a religion of their own and have a country of their own in which they could feed themselves, clothe themselves, and shelter themselves.

CLARK: In fact then, you're saying that the Black Muslim movement——

MALCOLM X: It's not a Black Muslim movement.

CLARK: All right, then——

MALCOLM X: We are black people who are Muslims because we believe in the religion of Islam.

CLARK: ——this movement which you so ably represent actually desires separation.

MALCOLM X: Complete separation; not only physical separation but moral separation. This is why the Honorable Elijah Muhammad teaches the black people in this country that we must stop drinking, we must stop smoking, we must stop committing fornication and adultery, we must stop gambling and cheating and using profanity, we must stop showing disrespect for our women, we must reform our-selves as parents so we can set the proper example for our children. Once we reform ourselves of these immoral habits, that makes us more godly, more godlike, more righteous. That means we are qualified then, to be on God's side, and it puts God on our side. God becomes our champion then, and it makes it possible for us to accomplish our own aims.

CLARK: This movement then, is not particularly sympa-thetic with the integrationist goals of the N.A.A.C.P., C.O.R.E., Martin Luther King, and the student non-violent movement.

MALCOLM X: Mister Muhammad teaches us that integra-tion is only a trick on the part of the white man today to lull Negroes to sleep, to lull them into thinking that the white man is changing and actually trying to keep us here; but America itself, because of the seeds that it has sown in the past against the black man, is getting ready to reap the whirlwind today, reap the harvest. Just as Egypt had to pay for its crime that it committed for enslaving the Hebrews, the Honorable Elijah Muhammad teaches us that America has to pay today for the crime that is committed in enslaving the so-called Negroes.

CLARK: There is one question that has bothered me a great deal about your movement, and it involves just a little incident. Rockwell, who is a self-proclaimed white supremacist and American Nazi, was given an honored front row position at one of your——

MALCOLM X: This is incorrect.

CLARK: Am I wrong?

MALCOLM X: This is a false statement that has been put out by the press. And Jews have used it to spread anti-Muslim propaganda throughout this country. Mister Muhammad had an open convention to which he invited anyone, black and white. (And this is another reason why we keep white people out of our meetings.) He invited everyone, both black and white, and Rockwell came. Rockwell came the same as any other white person came, and when we took up a collection, we called out the names of everyone who made a donation. Rockwell's name was called out the same as anybody else's, and this was projected to make it look like Rockwell was financing the Muslims. And secondly, Rockwell came to another similar meeting. At this meeting Mister Muhammad gave anyone who wanted to oppose him or congratulate him an opportunity to speak. Rockwell spoke; he was not even allowed up on the rostrum; he spoke from a microphone from which other whites spoke at the same meeting. And again the Jewish press, or the Jewish who are a part of the press—Jewish *people* who are part of the press—used this as propaganda to make it look like Rockwell was in cahoots with the Muslims. Rockwell, to us, is no different from any other white man. One of the things that I *will* give Rockwell credit for: he preaches and practices the same thing. And these other whites running around here posing as liberals, patting Negroes on the back—they think the same thing that Rockwell thinks, only they speak a different talk, a different language.

CLARK: Minister Malcolm, you have mentioned the Jews and the Jewish press and Jewish propaganda frequently in this discussion. It has been said frequently that an important part of your movement is anti-Semitism. I have seen you deny this.

MALCOLM X: No. We're a——

CLARK: Would you want to comment on this?

MALCOLM X: No, the followers of Mister Muhammad aren't anti-anything but anti-wrong, anti-exploitation and anti-oppression. A lot of the Jews have a guilty conscience when you mention exploitation because they realize that they control ninety per cent of the businesses in every Negro community from the Atlantic to the Pacific and that they get more benefit from the Negro's purchasing power than the Negro himself does or than any other white or any other segment of the white community does, so they have a guilt complex on this. And whenever you mention exploitation of Negroes, most Jews think that you're talking about them, and in order to hide what they are guilty of, they accuse you of being anti-Semitic.

CLARK: Do you believe the Jews are more guilty of this exploitation than are——

MALCOLM X: Jews belong to practically every Negro organization Negroes have. Arthur T. Spingarn, the head of the N.A.A.C.P., is Jewish. Every organization that Negroes—— When I say the head of the N.A.A.C.P., the *president* of the N.A.A.C.P. is Jewish. The same Jews wouldn't let you become the president of the B'nai B'rith or their different organizations.

CLARK: Thank you very much. You have certainly presented important parts of your movement, your point of view. I think we understand more clearly now some of your goals, and I'd like to know if we could talk some other time if you would tell me a little about what you think is the future of the Negro in America other than separation.

MALCOLM X: Yes. As long as they have interviews with the Attorney General and take Negroes to pose as leaders, all of whom are married either to white men or white women, you'll always have a race problem. When Baldwin took that crew with him to see Kennedy, he took the wrong crew. And as long as they take the wrong crew to talk to that man, you're not going to get anywhere near any solution to this problem in this country.

Martin Luther King

talks with

Kenneth B. Clark

Martin Luther King was interviewed on a day when he had already spent three hours taping another television program. When we called for him at his hotel, he seemed weary, but desirous of hiding this fact. On the way to the studio, we talked generally about developments on the various civil-rights fronts. He seemed particularly optimistic that a solid and workable agreement was going to be implemented in Birmingham. His tone before the interview was the same as his tone during the interview—a calm, quiet, confident belief in the future.

This observer has no doubts that Martin Luther King's philosophy of love for the oppressor is a genuine aspect of his being. He personally does not differentiate between this philosophy and the effectiveness of the non-violent direct-action approach to the attainment of racial justice, which he personifies and leads. For him, the philosophy is not just a strategy; it is a truth, it is his assertion of the philosophical position that one cannot differentiate means from ends. The quiet, contemplative, at times exasperatingly academic style is truly King. He is the paradox of the scholar and the effective man of social action.

Martin Luther King is a quietly pleasant young man. There is little about his personal appearance that suggests the firm, courageous leader of public demonstrations. There is no way that one could tell by looking at him that he has exposed himself repeatedly to death, and that by sheer force of his personality and the depth of his convictions, has moved the South and the North. He is the embodiment of that dignity which is essential for every man.

CLARK: In December of 1955 an event in Montgomery, Alabama, catapulted a young man into national and international prominence. The Reverend Martin Luther King, Jr., led the effective Montgomery bus boycott wherein the Negro people of that city stated for the entire world the fact that they were no longer content with second-class citizenship. Since that time Doctor King has personified that dignity, that discipline, and that insistence upon the rights of an American citizen which the present thrust of the Negro people represents. Doctor King, I know that people throughout America have watched your leadership in the Birmingham situation. Before we talk about those problems which have gotten the headlines and coverage in all our mass media, I'd like to know a little about you as a person. Where were you born? Something about your family, brothers and sisters, and things of that sort.

KING: Yes. Well, I was born in the South, in Atlanta, Georgia, and I lived there all of my early years. In fact, I went to the public schools of Atlanta and I went to college in Atlanta. I left after college to attend theological school.

CLARK: What college did you go to?

KING: Morehouse College in Atlanta.

CLARK: Part of the Atlanta University system.

KING: That's right. And I was raised in the home of a minister; my father pastors the Ebenezer Church in Atlanta and has pastored this church for thirty-three years. I am now co-pastor of the same church with him. And we have— I mean there's a family of three children in the immediate family; I have one brother and one sister.

CLARK: Is your brother a pastor also?

KING: Yes, he is. He's the pastor of the First Baptist Church of Birmingham, Alabama.

CLARK: And you have a sister?

KING: Yes, she's in Atlanta, teaching at Spelman College.

CLARK: Now, about your own immediate family: I remember the last time we were together in Montgomery you had a son who had just been born before the Montgomery disturbances.

KING: Well, that was a daughter. The second child was a son, but our first child was a daughter. Since that time we've had two more, so we have four children now, two sons and two daughters, the most recent one being the daughter that came nine weeks ago.

CLARK: How wonderful. It seems as if you have children at times of major crises.

KING: Yes, that's right, and that brings new life to life.

CLARK: Very good. You went from Morehouse to Boston University to study philosophy, am I correct?

KING: Well, no, I went from Morehouse to Crozer Theological Seminary in Pennsylvania and then I went from Crozer to Boston University.

CLARK: In Boston you studied philosophy and, if I remember correctly, you have a Ph.D. in philosophy.

KING: Well, the actual field is philosophical theology.

CLARK: Now, if we could shift a little from the education within the academic halls to your education in the community. I look at our newspapers and see that you have not only engaged in and led many of these demonstrations, but have paid for this by seeing the inside of many jails. I've wondered—how many jails have you been to as a result of your involvement in this direct-action, non-violent insistence upon the rights of Negroes?

KING: Well, I've been arrested fourteen times since we started out in Montgomery. Some have been in the same jail, that is, I've been in some jails more than once. I haven't calculated the number of different jails. I would say about eight of them were different jails. I remember once within eight days I transferred to three different jails within the state of Georgia. I think I've been to about eight different jails and I've been arrested about fourteen times.

CLARK: Have you attempted to make a study of these jails, for example, the type of jail, the type of individuals you've met in these jails as keepers, say, or wardens? What type of human beings are these or are they different types of human beings?

KING: Well, I have gone through the process of comparing the various jails. I guess this is one of those inevitable things that you find yourself doing to kind of lift yourself from the dull monotony of sameness when you're in jail and I find that they do differ. I've been in some new jails and I've been in some mighty old ones. In the recent jail experience in Birmingham I was in the new jail. The city jail is about a year old, I think, and in Albany, Georgia, last year I was in a very old jail. In Fulton County, Georgia, I was in a very new one.

CLARK: What about the human beings who are the jail-keepers? What about their attitude toward you as a person?

KING: Well, they vary also. I have been in jails where the jailers were exceptionally courteous and they went out of their way to see that everything went all right where I was concerned. On the other hand, I have been in jails where the jailers were extremely harsh and vitriolic in their words and in their manners. I haven't had any experience of physical violence from jailers, but I have had violence of words from them. Even in Birmingham, for the first few days, some of the jailers were extremely harsh in their statements.

CLARK: Have you ever been in an integrated jail? In the South?

KING: No, that's one experience I haven't had yet.

CLARK: Well, maybe after we get through integrating public accommodations the last thing will be to integrate the jailhouses.

KING: Yes.

CLARK: I am very much interested in the philosophy of

non-violence and particularly I would like to understand more clearly for myself the relationship between the direct-action non-violence technique which you have used so effectively and your philosophy of, for want of better words I'll use, "love of the oppressor."

KING: All right.

CLARK: Doctor King, what do you see as the relationship between these two things, which could be seen as separate?

KING: Yes, I think so. One is a method of action: non-violent direct action is a method of acting to rectify a social situation that is unjust and it involves in engaging in a practical technique that nullifies the use of violence or calls for non-violence at every point. That is, you don't use physical violence against the opponent. Now, the love ethic is another dimension which goes into the realm of accepting non-violence as a way of life. There are many people who will accept non-violence as the most practical technique to be used in a social situation, but they would not go to the point of seeing the necessity of accepting non-violence as a way of life. Now, I accept both. I think that non-violent resistance is the most potent weapon available to oppressed people in their struggle for freedom and human dignity. It has a way of disarming the opponent. It exposes his moral defenses. It weakens his morale and at the same time it works on his conscience. He just doesn't know how to handle it and I have seen this over and over again in our struggle in the South. Now on the question of love or the love ethic, I think this is so important because hate is injurious to the hater as well as the hated. Many of the psychiatrists are telling us now that many of the strange things that happen in the subconscious and many of the inner conflicts are rooted in hate and so they are now saying "love or perish." Eric Fromm can write a book like *The Art of Loving* and make it very clear that love is the supreme unifying principle of life and I'm trying to say in this movement that it is necessary to follow the technique of non-violence as the most potent weapon available to us, but it is necessary also to follow the love ethic which becomes a force of personality integration.

CLARK: But is it not too much to expect that a group of human beings who have been the victims of cruelty and flagrant injustice could actually love those who have been associated with the perpetrators, if not the perpetrators themselves? How could you expect, for example, the Negroes in Birmingham who know Bull Connor to really love him in any meaningful sense?

KING: Well, I think one has to understand the meaning of "love" at this point. I'm certainly not speaking of an affectionate response. I think it is really nonsense to urge oppressed peoples to love their oppressors in an affectionate sense. And I often call on the Greek language to aid me at this point because there are three words in the Greek for "love." One is "eros," which is sort of an aesthetic or a romantic love. Another is "fileo," which is sort of an intimate affection between personal friends; this is friendship, it is a reciprocal love and on this level, you love those people that you like. And then the Greek language comes out with the word "agape," which is understanding, creative, redemptive good will for all men. It goes far beyond an affectionate response. Now when I say to you——

CLARK: That form means really understanding.

KING: Yes, that's right. And you come to the point of being able to love the person that does an evil deed in the sense of understanding and you can hate the deed that the person does. And I'm certainly not talking about "eros"; I'm not talking about friendship. I find it pretty difficult to like people like Bull Connor. I find it difficult to like Senator Eastman, but I think you can love where you can't like the person because life is an affectionate quality.

CLARK: Yes, I have admired your ability to feel this, and I must say to you also that as I read your expounding of the philosophy of love I found myself often feeling personally quite inadequate. Malcolm X, one of the most articulate exponents of the Black Muslim philosophy, has said of your movement and your philosophy that it plays into the hands of the white oppressors, that they are happy to hear you talk about love for the oppressor because this disarms the Negro and fits into the stereotype of the Negro as a meek, turning-the-other-cheek sort of creature. Would you care to comment on Mister X's beliefs?

KING: Well, I don't think of love, as in this context, as emotional bosh. I don't think of it as a weak force, but I think of love as something strong and that organizes itself into powerful direct action. Now, this is what I try to teach in this struggle in the South: that we are not engaged in a struggle that means we sit down and do nothing; that there is a great deal of difference between non-resistance to evil and non-violent resistance. Non-resistance leaves you in a state of stagnant passivity and deadly complacency where non-violent resistance means that you do resist in a very strong and determined manner and I think some of the criticisms of non-violence or some of the critics fail to realize that we are talking about something very strong and they confuse non-resistance with non-violent resistance.

CLARK: *He* goes beyond that in some of the things I've heard him say—to say that this is deliberately your philosophy of love of the oppressor which he identifies completely with the non-violent movement. He says this philosophy and this movement are actually encouraged by whites because it makes them comfortable. It makes them believe that Negroes are meek, supine creatures.

KING: Well, I don't think that's true. If anyone has ever lived with a non-violent movement in the South, from Mont-

gomery on through the freedom rides and through the sit-in
movement and the recent Birmingham movement and seen
the reactions of many of the extremists and reactionaries in
the white community, he wouldn't say that this movement
makes—this philosophy makes them comfortable. I think it
arouses a sense of shame within them often—in many in-
stances. I think it does something to touch the conscience
and establish a sense of guilt. Now so often people respond
to guilt by engaging more in the guilt-evoking act in an
attempt to drown the sense of guilt, but this approach
certainly doesn't make the white man feel comfortable. I
think it does the other thing. It disturbs his conscience and
it disturbs this sense of contentment that he's had.

CLARK: James Baldwin raises still another point of the
whole non-violent position, an approach. He does not reject
it in the ways that Malcolm X does, but he raises the question of whether it will be possible to contain the Negro
people within this framework of non-violence if we continue
to have more of the kinds of demonstrations that we had in
Birmingham, wherein police brought dogs to attack human
beings. What is your reaction to Mr. Baldwin's anxiety?

KING: Well, I think these brutal methods used by the
Birmingham police force and other police forces will naturally arouse the ire of Negroes and I think there is the danger
that some will be so aroused that they will retaliate with
violence. I think though that we can be sure that the vast
majority of Negroes who engage in the demonstrations and
who understand the non-violent philosophy will be able to
face dogs and all of the other brutal methods that are used
without retaliating with violence because they understand
that one of the first principles of non-violence is the willingness to be the recipient of violence while never inflicting
violence upon another. And none of the demonstrators in
Birmingham engaged in aggressive or retaliatory violence.
It was always someone on the sideline who had never been

in the demonstrations and probably not in the mass meetings and had never been in a non-violent workshop. So I think it will depend on the extent to which we can extend the teaching of the philosophy of non-violence to the larger community rather than those who are engaged in the demonstrations.

CLARK: Well, how do you maintain this type of discipline, control and dignity in your followers who do participate in the demonstrations? You don't have police force, you have no uniform, you're not an authoritarian organization, you're a group of people who are voluntarily associated. How do you account for this, I would say, beautiful dignity and discipline?

KING: Well, we do a great deal in terms of teaching both the theoretical aspects of non-violence as well as the practical application. We even have courses where we go through the experience of being roughed up and this kind of socio-drama has proved very helpful in preparing those who are engaged in demonstrations. The other thing is——

CLARK: Does this even include the children?

KING: Yes, it includes the children. In Birmingham where we had several young—we had some as young as seven years old to participate in the demonstrations, and they were in the workshops. In fact, none of them went out for a march, none of them engaged in any of the demonstrations before going through this kind of teaching session. So that through this method we are able to get the meaning of non-violence over, and I think there is a contagious quality in a movement like this when everybody talks about non-violence and being faithful to it and being dignified in your resistance. It tends to get over to the larger group because this becomes a part of the vocabulary of the movement.

CLARK: What is the relationship between your movement and such organizations as the N.A.A.C.P., C.O.R.E. and the

Student Non-violent Coordinating Committee? They're separate organizations, but do you work together?

KING: Yes, we do. As you say, each of these organizations
is autonomous, but we work together in many, many ways.
Last year we started a voter-registration drive, an intensified
voter-registration drive. And all of the organizations are
working together, sometimes two or three are working together in the same community. The same thing is true with
our direct-action programs. In Birmingham we had the support of Snick and C.O.R.E. and the N.A.A.C.P. C.O.R.E.
sent some of its staff members in to assist us and Snick sent
some of its staff members. Roy Wilkins came down to speak
in one of the mass meetings and to make it clear that even
though the N.A.A.C.P. cannot operate in Alabama, we had
the support of the N.A.A.C.P. So that we are all working together in a very significant way, and we are doing even more
in the days ahead to co-ordinate our efforts.

CLARK: Is there any machinery—does machinery for co-
ordination actually exist now?

KING: Well, we have had a sort of co-ordinating council
where we get together as often as possible. Of course, we get
involved in many of our programs in the various areas and
can't make as many of these meetings as we would like but
we often come together (I mean, the heads of all these organizations) to try to co-ordinate our various efforts.

CLARK: What about the Federal government? Have you
made any direct appeal either in your own right or as part
of this leadership group to have a more active involvement
in the Federal government in the rights of Negroes?

KING: Yes, I have. I've made appeals and other members
of the Southern Christian Leadership Conference have appealed to the President and the new administration generally
to do more in dealing with the problem of racial injustice.
I think Mister Kennedy has done some significant things in

civil rights, but I do not feel that he has yet given the leadership that the enormity of the problem demands.

CLARK: By Mister Kennedy, now, do you mean the President?

KING: Yes, I'm speaking now of the President, mainly.
And I would include the Attorney General. I think both of
these men are men of genuine good will, but I think they
must understand more about the depths and dimensions of
the problem and I think there is a necessity now to see the
urgency of the moment. There isn't a lot of time; time is
running out, and the Negro is making it palpably clear that
he wants all of his rights, that he wants them here, and that
he wants them now.

CLARK: Is this not considered by some people an ex-
tremist position, that is, not really practical?

KING: Yes, I'm sure many people feel this, but I think
they must see the truth of the situation. The shape of the
world today does not afford us the luxury of slow movement
and the Negro's quest for dignity and self-respect doesn't
afford the nation this kind of slow movement.

CLARK: Doctor King, what do you think will be the out-
come of the present confrontation, the present insistence of
the Negroes for their rights as American citizens without
equivocation and without qualification? Do you think this
will be obtained?

KING: I do. Realism impels me to admit that there will
be difficult days ahead. In some of the hard-core states in
the South we will confront resistance. There will still be resistance and there will still be very real problems in the
North as a result of the twin evils of employment and hous-
ing discrimination, but I think there are forces at work now
that will somehow ward off all of these ominous possibilities.
The rolling tide of world opinion will play a great part in
this. I think the aroused conscience of many, many white

people all over the country, the growing awareness of religious institutions that they have not done their job, and
the determination of the Negro himself, and the growing
industrialization in the South—all of these things, I believe
—will conjoin to make it possible for us to move on toward
the goal of integration.

CLARK: So you are hopeful?

KING: Yes, I am.

CLARK: And I thank you for your hope and I thank you
for your actions.

KING: Thank you.

Differences and Similarities

by

Kenneth B. Clark

When one looks at these interviews certain differences and some striking similarities emerge. The differences seem fairly obvious, and apparently easy to understand. James Baldwin, a passionate, anguished writer and intellectual, tries desperately to reach the conscience of America. He looks, and he critically appraises the philosophy and the methods of Elijah Muhammad and the Black Muslims. He tries to understand the depth of despair from which these over-simplified views and methods spring. Baldwin looks with equal candor at Martin Luther King and wonders aloud whether the philosophy of love is sufficient to contain the restless impatience of the masses of Negroes. Like the artist of all times and all groups, Baldwin is essentially alone. He cannot have the stabilizing support of a group for which he is responsible or to which he belongs. He must belong only to the validity of his ideas. Each time I have talked with Baldwin, personally or publicly, I am left with the feeling that he is a delicately tuned instrument of pure communication. The value of Baldwin's role, and the burden which he cannot avoid, is that this skill be used to awaken the conscience of America.

Malcolm X is clear. His answers come directly from the source of all knowledge, Elijah Muhammad or Allah. He knows what must be done. He knows that the white man and the Jew are devils, and that the black man alone is the soul of virtue. He need not be anguished by the complexities inherent in transforming our society to one of racial equality and peace. The answer for Minister Malcolm is complete separation. One of the few areas of vagueness for him is when he is required to deal with the crucial question of separation to what, and how, and when. It is not enough for us to say that the answers of

the Black Muslims lead only to blind alleys. The followers of
Elijah Muhammad do not appear to be as much concerned with
the attainment of goals as they are with the exploitation of
grievances. And the grievances are real! This is the basis of
Malcolm X's appeal.

Martin Luther King speaks as a committed Christian. He
insists that Negroes seek equality through disciplined non-violence. He seems free to impose this burden upon his fellow-
sufferers because he has demonstrated that he has accepted it
himself. Apparently unmoved by questions concerning the realism or the relevance of his philosophy, he contents himself with
demonstrating the effectiveness of his methods.

Each of these three men reflects in his being the quest of
all Negroes for a positive identity, a recognition and respect
for their individuality, and an insistence upon their total humanity. The very differences in their approach—the paradox
of Malcolm X's cry for separation in contrast to Martin
Luther King's insistence upon integration—reflect the Negro's
assertion that America must learn to accept him as an individual with the same broad spectrum of individual differences
which are found in all other groups.

If one dares to probe beneath the surface of the various
forms of the present Negro protest to find the common compel-
ling force, one will probably find that it is a rather simple and
universal human desire. It is the desire to be respected for one's
self—the desire to be seen and to be reacted to as an individual human being; the desire to be free of the shackles of being
lumped, categorized, and stigmatized as an inchoate mass. The
Negro has no more or less virtues or frailities than those found
in other human beings. He is an individual who varies as much
in courage and cowardice or ambivalence as do other human
beings. He reacts to injustices and cruelties with the same pat-
terns of accommodation, intimidation, rebellion, or philosophy

as do others. He is here. Like others, throughout his life, he is in a relentless struggle against the void, the inner chaos. He is an individual. If life is to be tolerable for him he must be respected as an individual.

A Note About the Interviews

A Note About the Interviews

by Henry Morgenthau III

The three interviews in *The Negro Protest* were recorded for television in May and June of 1963. Dr. Kenneth Clark and I invited the comments of Reverend Martin Luther King, Jr. and Minister Malcolm X because they stood at opposite ends of the spectrum of opinion. King was just then being heralded as the hero of the Birmingham demonstrations. He was the symbol of the non-violent, direct-action struggle for integration and immediate achievement of full rights. Malcolm X presented a kind of alternative. As the Black Muslims' most eloquent spokesman, he was the apostle of black racism and complete separation, and appealed to the most alienated Negroes. James Baldwin, although not a leader in the traditional sense, was invited as the writer and poet most sensitive to the Negro protest.

The Baldwin interview, as Clark has noted, was recorded on May 24, 1963, following the meeting with the Attorney General, Robert Kennedy, and a group of friends and associates Baldwin had assembled. Realizing that the Baldwin-Clark interview was an exciting footnote to this historic confrontation, we decided to broadcast it four days later on May 28, well in advance of the date scheduled for the completed three-part program. As Jack Gould pointed out in the New York *Times,* we had "achieved an 'exclusive' that underscored the inadequacy of the networks in covering the meeting between the Negro leaders and Mr. Kennedy. . . . What an admirable goal for educational TV: to hit hard and consistently in the resolution of the hour's foremost moral issue. . . ." He went on to say, "That instant when the writer [Baldwin] starkly challenged members of the audience to put humanity before his color or theirs was a moment of truth that did not end with the program." Now it seems important to many of us that the full range and force of this mounting wave of Negro protest, captured only fleetingly on television, be preserved in print.

The interviews published here were recorded for a television program entitled "The Negro and the American Promise" which I produced for the National Educational Television and Radio Center with the staff and facilities of the Boston educational station WGBH-TV. The form of the program and *The Negro Protest* are slightly different, although both have the unifying thread and style provided by Dr. Clark's method of interviewing his subjects and his personal concept of the Negro protest. It was, above all, his skill and modesty as an interviewer, and the respect he commanded on the part of the three men, which caused them to respond so fully and freely. For me the privilege of working with Kenneth Clark and learning from him was very rewarding. I originally found my way to Dr. Clark at the suggestion of Samuel Allen of the United States Information Agency and Marvin Rich of the Congress of Racial Equality. To both I am most grateful.

I have reserved the final and very special expression of gratitude to my two WGBH teammates, Mary Rose Maybank, co-producer, and Fred Barzyk, director, without whose talent and friendship the television program would never have been.